I0519273

ELIMINATING BARRIERS

POCKET EDITION

Published from
Mardukite Borsippa HQ, San Luis Valley, Colorado
Mardukite Academy & Systemology Society
for spiritual or educational purposes only

ELIMINATING BARRIERS

Systemology
Professional Course
Booklet #7

Developed by Joshua Free
for the Systemology Society

THE JOSHUA FREE IMPRINT
JFI PUBLICATIONS

© 2023, JOSHUA FREE

ISBN : 978-1-961509-31-3

Pocket Paperback Edition — *November 2023*

mardukite.com

Chart Your Flight For Ascension...
Then Let Your Spirit Fly!

Unlock your ultimate spiritual potential by removing barriers to your true native state.

Learn how to easily attain Self-actualization and help to actualize others along the way.

A greater appreciation and understanding of *Spiritual Life* and *Existence* awaits you. Expand your reach to achieve your dreams.

Each 'Professional Course' lesson-booklet offers simple exercises and techniques that directly apply the philosophy of Systemology, assisting to increase your true knowingness, improve your capabilities in this life, and even decide what you will do in your next.

At the Mardukite Academy of Systemology, the 'Professional Course' lessons in this series are presented to Seeker's that have already completed the 'Basic Course', previously released as six lesson-booklets, or the six-in-one single volume edition "Fundamentals of Systemology."

This all new presentation of the Systemology 'Pathway-to-Ascension' takes Seekers and continuing students from "Zero" to "Infinity" at lightning-fast speeds!

Discover Who You Really Are...

Because You Were Never Human

TABLET OF CONTENTS

COURSE INTRODUCTION

LESSON SEVEN: ELIMINATING BARRIERS

APPENDIX

PROFESSIONAL COURSE INTRODUCTION

WELCOME, SEEKER!
LET'S CHART YOUR JOURNEY
ON THE PATHWAY

Systemology is a "holistic" approach to understanding the human experience. It is not actually a singular "subject" in itself, but rather, a new way in which to view the many subjects of *Life* and all *Existence*.

This is a professional course in *Systemology*—specifically, how to *apply* the spiritual philosophy of *Mardukite Systemology* as a personal *"Pathway" to Ascension*. Our *Systemology* is a new approach to *"Self-Actualization."* It is completely relevant for the modern age and the future; and quite different from any previous similar attempts, or other traditions, you might find. What's more: it is applicable to anyone with any background.

This *"Professional Course"* series of lessons (booklets) immediately follows the material given in the *"Basic Course"* series—available as six separate pocket-sized booklets, or in a single hardcover volume titled: *"Fundamentals of Systemology: A New Thought For The 21st Century."*

This is a *new* presentation of *Systemology*, emphasizing the application of our philosophy for those *Seekers* that are *"Flying-Solo"*—or else working through their studies and exercises as solitary practitioners. This is a new innovation for *Systemology*. Aside from the book *"Crystal Clear,"* all of our former advanced courses have placed a focus on *"Traditional Piloting"*—where experienced practitioners assist *Seekers* in *"processing."*

To receive the greatest benefit from this study: it is expected that a *Seeker* will already be familiar with the fundamental concepts and terminology (previously relayed in the *Basic Course*) before using lessons from the *Professional Course*. This will allow us to cover the extensive territory of the *Pathway* much more quickly. However, for reference, a basic "*glossary*" of vocabulary used in this lesson is provided in the "*appendix*."

A NEW VIEW OF THE HUMAN SPIRIT

Systemology is not a religion and does not require any type of *faith*. It is, however, built upon a "spiritual" premise—and as such is an "applied spiritual philosophy." It is based on ancient teachings that we are *Spiritual Beings* essentially "wearing" bodies like clothes—or using them as "vehicles." Yet our true native nature is not *physical,* but beyond this existence; and we can certainly operate a "body" from *outside* of it.

13

We are **all** *Spiritual Beings*—each of us a *unit* of *Spiritual Awareness*—that have experienced a very long *Spiritual Timeline* of existence. Although we might be particularly attached to the familiar "physical shells" associated with *this* lifetime, our true *"Spiritual Lifetime"* is seemingly *eternal*. We have been many things before *Human*, and we go onward as a *Spiritual Being* after our *"genetic vehicle"* of *this* incarnation perishes.

While a "spiritual" view of the *Human Condition* may not seem unique to our philosophy, just how often is the concept treated *systematically*? For that matter: just how many people, supposedly raised to this or that religion, or professing to believe one thing or another, actually live their lives as though they are *Spirits?*

As *Spiritual Beings* of immortal existence and infinite potential, we are not simply the *"creations"* of an even greater *Being-*

ness; we are, in fact, an integral part of that *"creative force"* which permeates all existence.

Our basic nature is to be a *"creative being"*—our highest goals are *"to create."* And as such a being—which we refer to as an *Alpha-Spirit* in *Systemology*—we have run into some difficulties along the course of our *Spiritual Timeline* and found ourselves trapped within material *Universes* of our own collaborative *creation*.

Since we did not start out our existence in a trapped condition, it is correct to say that we have *"fallen"* from our native *"godlike"* states. It did not happen all at one, but progressively and systematically. We know our "troubles" have resulted from accumulated "barriers" and "blockages"—or *fragmentation*—during our vast experiences as *Spiritual Beings*. They are not because we lack something; but because of what's been added.

15

In *Systemology*, we systematically examine those routes by which we must have descended to reach our present condition, then reverse the direction of travel and chart a personal *"Pathway to Ascension."* Of course, the exact "details" of the *Spiritual Timeline* will be different for each individual *Seeker*. However, we have been able to systematically chart our *Pathway* based on common patterns of *Human fragmentation*.

In the most basic terms: the *fragmentation* that defines our "downward spiral" consists of decisions or considerations where we deny our true nature. This includes those decisions to *"withdraw"* rather than *"reach"*; where we choose to *not-know* rather than *know*; to *not-communicate* rather than *communicate*; and ultimately, to take *no-responsibility* for being a *creative-cause*, and therefore succumb to being an *effect*.

But there is *hope!* And much more importantly: there is an effectively workable *way out* of the mazes and traps of our existence. If you are reading this now, you have already begun to gather your tools and build up the *"horsepower"* necessary to break the gravity holding your *Spiritual Beingness* to the *Human Condition.*

STUDYING THE PROFESSIONAL COURSE

Most *Seekers* study and practice *Systemology* at-a-distance and independent of the "Mardukite Academy" or any "Master-level" mentors trained therein. This means that the *books* (and to a lesser degree, the *internet*) are the only means of direct contact a *Seeker* maintains with the "Systemology Society" during their studies. A continuing *Seeker* from the *"Basic Course"* will be familiar with the style of study found in *this* course.

17

Misunderstood words are the most common reason an individual abandons studying a subject. When a misunderstanding occurs, *Awareness* declines. These misunderstandings start to "stack up" after the first occurrence, and as a result, the level of interest and attention will also decline. This is how a "confusion" develops; and the individual will get "bored" with the subject, feel tired, and unable to concentrate.

One solution is to return to the part of the material that was still interesting and enjoyable to read. When scanning around that area of text, there is likely to be a new word (or new specific use of a familiar word) that is unclear, but was passed by unnoticed. All *Systemology* books include their own *glossary*. Using this *glossary* and a high-quality dictionary will help resolve this misunderstanding once it is located.

An effective education of any subject is taught on a *gradient*. This is what is intended by presenting the study of something as *"grades."* Rather than treating a subject as one total mass, true learning is achieved by increasing one's understanding with a *gradual* increase upward. The *ascent* to a mountaintop is not successfully achieved in one leap, but by targeting and reaching specific checkpoints along the way.

This *Professional Course* consists of a series of lessons (booklets) that gradually increase a *Seeker's* ability to understand and apply the practices and techniques of *Systemology* as a complete *"Pathway to Ascension."* It is an appropriate study for continuing *Seekers* (from the *Basic Course*), but also "advanced" *Systemologists*.

Each lesson (booklet) of the *Professional Course* applies *Systemology* to a particular subject (or focus). It is best if the entire course can be studied and applied in sequential order. These lessons also employ a style of practice or technique called *"Systematic Processing."* An introduction to applying this methodology is provided in the final lesson (booklet) of the *Basic Course*—or in the *"Fundamentals of Systemology"* volume.

To study the *Professional Course* just like a student at the Academy: a *Seeker* reads through all instructional material and applies each exercise (or *"process"*) presented in the text to the extent they comfortably can, before continuing on to the next lesson (booklet).

When first starting on the *Pathway* as a *Solo* practitioner, without the aid of an experienced *Pilot*, a *Seeker* shouldn't "push too hard" or allow themselves to get too "stuck" on any one area (lesson) or *process*. It is not expected that any one area will be completely handled when first introduced. For optimum results, it is expected that a serious *Seeker* will make more than one "pass" through the entire *Professional Course.*

The *Professional Course* is not altogether different from other forms of practical or technical education: where the instruction and exercises are delivered to a completion, and then a student further increases their abilities, strength and skill-level by applying additional practice throughout their life. Therefore, a student should not concern themselves with perfectly mastering each step (or lesson) before progressing forward.

Additional passes through the material are likely to result in different *"realizations"* (an increased *level of understanding*) than a previous time. New "layers" of *Knowingness* may now be accessible during a *process* that may not have been before. It is important to avoid invalidating the progress you've made just because one area is not completely handled right away, or if a certain *process* seems too difficult on the first pass.

CHARTING A COURSE ON THE PATHWAY

Although we can communicate a systematic structure to *fragmentation,* the personal journey experienced along the *Pathway* will be different for each *Seeker.* For example, certain areas will seem more "*turbulent*" or difficult for one *Seeker* than another. We tend to say that these areas have more "*charge*" on them—or that they are more "*heavily charged.*" It is best to handle such areas when you are already feeling "good" and not in a situation (or condition) where that specific area is consistently being "*triggered*" or "*restimulated.*"

As an applied philosophy, *Systemology* "theory" can be easily utilized in the "laboratory" of the "world-at-large" in everyday life. This is implied within the basic instruction of each lesson. Unlike other "sciences" that conduct experiments by making a change to some "objective variable" *out there* and waiting to see an effect, our focus is the individual (or *Observer*) themselves, and how *they* affect the "*Reality*" perceived.

In addition to applying *Systemology* "New Thought" to everyday life, our philosophy is applied by using specific exercises and systematic techniques. These "*processes*" provide the most stable personal gain (and *realizations*) for each area; but only when actually applied with a *Seeker's* full "*presence*" and *Awareness*.

This *Professional Course* is designed so that it may be easily read and studied with little concern for what "dangers" these teachings—or *processing*—might unleash. However, there are still some guidelines that pertain to the "best-uses" of these course lessons, particularly if a *Seeker* intends for stable development.

Skipping over too much material/*processing* in early lessons may make attempts to understand (or apply) later lessons more difficult. However, once the complete *Professional Course* is worked through at least once in its entirety, specific areas can then be later returned to and treated with a greater sense of *Awareness* and *"presence"* than before. Of course, in *"Traditional Piloting,"* the rate of processing is monitored by an experienced practitioner; but in *"Solo-Processing,"* a *Seeker* must regulate their own progress on the *Pathway*.

Applying a systematic technique is called *"running a process."* The *processes* are designed with very simple instructions or "command-lines." To *run* a *processing command-line*, a *Seeker* may be assisted by the communication of that *line* from a "Co-Pilot" (as in *"Traditional Piloting"*). But even then, a *Seeker* must still personally "input" the *command* as *Self*. For this reason —and quite thankfully— *Solo-Processing* is possible.

TAKING FLIGHT ON THE PATHWAY

Processing Techniques are intended to treat the *Spiritual Being* or *Alpha-Spirit*; the individual themselves. It is applied by the *Alpha-Spirit*—then *Self-directed* to the "Mind-System" or even a "body" (*genetic-vehicle*), both of which are "constructs" that the *Alpha-Spirit* (*Self*, or the "I-AM" *Awareness unit*) operates, but neither of which is actually *Self*. *Fragmentation* causes *Humans* to falsely identify *Self as* the "*Mind*" or even a "*Body.*"

25

The *Professional Course* lessons (booklets) are designed for the *Beginning Seeker* in mind—one that may have an understanding of theory, but with little experience in practice. That being said: each of these lessons may be used toward total *Beta-Defragmentation* within a specific area. There are also more *processes* given for each subject than may be necessary to achieve an *ultimate end-point realization* on that entire area.

Some *processes* can be treated quite lightly at first; others may require a bit of working at in order to get *"running"* well. It is important to set aside a period of time when you can be dedicated to your studies and *processing.* This period of time is referred to as a *"processing session."* The reason for this, is that when a *process* does start *running* well, it is important to be able to complete it to a satisfactory *"end-point."*

The purpose of *systematic processing* is to be able to *really* "look" at things and even determine the *considerations* we have made—or attitudes we have decided—about *Reality* as a result of those experiences. It doesn't do us much good to simply "glance"—or to *restimulate* something uncomfortable and then quickly *withdraw* from it once again, leaving more of our *attention* yet again behind and held fixedly on it.

Generally speaking, a *Seeker* continues to *run* a *process* so long as something is "happening"—which is to say, the *process* is still producing a change. Usually this is evident by the type of "answers" that a *command-line* helps a *Seeker* originate from the database of their own *Mind-System*. The *command-lines* do not "do" anything on their own. They assist a *Seeker* to direct their own attention toward increasing *Awareness*.

27

Of course, a *Seeker* may also cease to generate new "data" from a *process* without reaching an *"ultimate" realization* as an *"end-point."* It is possible that additional "layers" (or even other "areas") require handling before anything "deeper" is accessible. If this is the case, end the *process*. But, if a *Seeker* is *withdrawing* from something uncomfortable that was incited or stirred up, then a *process* is *run* until they feel "good" about it.

In case the thought of encountering *"turbulence"* is a concern: the techniques given as *"Opening Procedures"* of a *Formal Session* (in the *Basic Course*), and those found in the earliest lessons of the *Professional Course*, are quite useful when applied as "safety nets" for maintaining *Awareness* and *presence*, even when *Flying-Solo*.

One of the benefits to *Flying-Solo* is that *processing* is entirely *Self-determined*. This already provides a certain built-in "safety" for a practitioner. Anything you *restimulate* by *Self-determinism* is *your thing*. It is not incited by external *other-determined* influences (or other "source-points" in existence) that make you an *effect*. It can be more easily handled in *processing*—or you can simply let things "cool down" and come back to it again.

While it may seem "mysterious" to beginners, a *Seeker* gets a sense for knowing how long to *run* a *process* only with practice. Once you have spent some time actually applying the *Professional Course*, there are many aspects that become "second nature" because they are, in fact, a part of our true original nature. All we have done is *"reverse engineer"* the routes of *creation* and *consideration* that are already *our own*.

LESSON SEVEN: ELIMINATING BARRIERS

GAMES AND BARRIERS

Participation in, and experience of, the Physical Universe (*"Beta Existence"*) is likened to a *"game"* in our *Systemology*. For philosophical and practical purposes, we apply *game theory* concepts to our *systematic processing* with regards to a *Seeker's* experience of *"Universes."* As such, an intellectual pursuit into *game theory* is of increasing interest to a *Seeker* as they progress along the *Pathway* (particularly at upper levels).

Perhaps the first thing that you should know about *"games"* is that they consist of certain *"rules"* or *"reality-agreements"* in order to functionally exist. In addition to an assigned *"space"* or *"game-field"* (or else, a *Shared Universe*) there are very specific *considerations* that define the *reality* of *"abilities"* (or *"freedoms"*) and *"purposes"* (or *"goals"*).

33

Reality-Agreements also define the *"barriers"* (*boundaries* and *obstacles*) that allow us to actually *have* a *game*. Unlimited freedom; no game. Unlimited barriers; no game. A lack of any purposes or goals; no game. So, for us to *have* any sense of a *"game"* in our lives, there are ultimately *"barriers"* in place that affect (or restrict, on an apparent level) our perceived *freedom* of play—meaning our *abilities* and *Knowingness*.

An *Alpha-Spirit* participates in *games* because it is something to *do*. We have all existed for a very long span of perceived *time* and have experienced countless different *Universes* along the way. We have also all *played* countless different *"roles"* during the course of our *Spiritual Existence*; made decisions based on perceived *"goals"* in each of these lifetimes. All of these aspects are considered within the domain of our *game theory*.

While our application of *game theory* reoccurs frequently in later *processing levels*, our present concern (when first entering *Systemology Level-3*) is specifically the subject of *barriers.* This lesson (booklet) directly continues from the material given in the previous one, and its invitation for a *Seeker* to *"reach further."* We will begin with some *"upper-level"* Systemology philosophy.

FRAGMENTATION AND BARRIERS

When first engaging in *Shared Universes* (or *Games Universes*), an *Alpha-Spirit* *"agrees"* to the *"reality"* of certain *barriers* in order to participate in and experience a specific *"Game of Life."* These *"reality-agreements"* make the *barriers* seem more *solid* than they *actually* are, and seem more *real* than the very *agreements* and *considerations* themselves that compose them.

During one's lifetime, an individual gets to believing that there are even more *barriers* than there are—and this is even the *esoteric* basis for dividing our perception of *ALL-Existence* into a series of "*veils*" or "*gates.*" For example: an individual believes they cannot *perceive, know,* or even *think* about certain things, because it somehow "goes beyond" or "exceeds" a certain *barrier*—even though that *barrier* does not actually exist.

Fragmented and low-*Awareness* states (that are typical of the *Human Condition*) allow an individual to falsely believe that the *barriers* and other "*game-mechanics*" are superior (or more solid/real) than the *agreements* and *considerations*; but "*games*" and "*barriers*" are really a "product of" *thoughts.* The *agreements* that compose the observable solidity of this *Universe* are really just a matter of "convenience" in order for us to have any kind of "shared" *reality* with others that are also experiencing this *Universe*.

The *"mechanics"* are simply solidified *"reality-agreements"* that provide an internal logic or consistent pattern for the *game* or *Universe*. Otherwise, consider three friends walking down a road: spontaneously, one turns into a tree; one disappears into a black-hole; and one simply sinks through the pavement, right through the earth, and into outer-space. Such *"randomness"* does not manifest on this planet because of agreed-upon *game-mechanics* inherent in the makeup and design of *this* specific *Universe* (*"Beta-Existence"*).

We *agreed* to the *game-mechanics* (of the *barriers*) so long ago that we have forgotten about it. *Fragmentation* leads us to believe that we are completely under the *effect* of these *"mechanics"* —and that this *Physical Universe* (or *Beta-Existence*) is somehow superior to our own true existence as *Alpha-Spirits*, when it is not.

But, these original *reality-agreements* were *"postulated"* into *existence* from a higher-level of *"Alpha-Thought."* They become quite solid by comparison to the level of *thought* and *consideration* available to the standard-issue *Human Condition*, which generally operates from a *viewpoint* "below" the level of those *agreements*. Thus, the "power" of *Human Thought* does not produce the same solid level of *effect* on one's environment.

It becomes quite apparent (from within our philosophy) that *fragmentation*, itself, is the only *real barrier*—and it is all that allows an *Alpha-Spirit* to get overwhelmed (or overpowered) by *Beta-Existence*, and believe *Self* to *be* something less than it actually is. This is what restricts an *Alpha-Spirit's* freedom and ability to fully "act" *within* the framework of the *game-mechanics*, when *Self* created and agreed to them in the first place.

In a state of *fragmentation*—such as the *Human Condition*—relatively "newer" *considerations* have less impact on the *mechanics* of the apparent "*Objective Universe*" than those *reality-agreements* made as "*Alpha-Thought.*" The "original" *agreements* are more "solid" in their apparent *reality* than "newer" *beliefs* and *considerations*. It is in this wise that an *Alpha-Spirit* became the *effect* of their own *creations*.

When an individual "*thinks*" or "*considers*" from a *viewpoint* within the *Human Condition*, they are running up against the very *game-mechanics* of *Beta-Existence*— and by this we mean very specifically: the high-level *agreements* an *Alpha-Spirit* has formerly made about *space-time* and *energy-matter* in this *Physical Universe*.

Some of the most basic *systematic processing* techniques (such as the "*objective processing*" exercises found throughout this *course* and in a *Formal Session*) are strongly effective because they put a

Seeker into such *clear communication* with the *Physical Universe* that they can more easily reclaim the *certainty, spiritual power,* and *creative ability* of their own original *"Alpha-Thought"* (*agreements* and *postulates*).

What is described within this section of our lesson is essentially the actual theory behind "opening procedures" and various techniques for establishing "presence in-session" used in formal *processing*.

For example: when a *Seeker* repeatedly (and *knowingly*) *"looks at"* and *"contacts the solidity"* of a *wall* that is in front of them with total *Awareness,* they *really* *"see"* the *wall* that *is* there *"As-It-Is"* (and often for the first time). [Refer to *Lesson-1,* *"Increasing Awareness,"* section titled: *"The Wall."*]

In essence, there is an "upper-level" *realization* available that *Self* has *created,* and is *agreeing* to, the *mechanics* of the *barrier*

40

on a continuous and compulsive basis. Once this is *recognized*, a *Seeker* can then begin to practice regaining the true "power" behind their *considerations*, and again have any high-level *control* (*"Alpha-Thought"*) over the actual *reality-agreements* and *mechanics* of a *Universe*.

PROCESSING "BARRIERS"

The *mechanics* of a *Shared/Game Universe* become such a point of inherent personal *fragmentation* that they act as apparent (or even visible) *"barriers"* — at least until the individual is again *able* to *be* free of them. It is not the *agreement* to have *barriers* and *games* that is problematic; the *fragmentation* occurs when the *Alpha-Spirit* is no longer *aware* of these *agreements*, yet continues to compulsively maintain their *reality*.

41

There are many times when it seems like certain applications of *systematic processing* shouldn't be necessary, since it should not be altogether difficult to "change your mind" about things. And if we could easily get an individual (entrapped within the *Human Condition*) to *actually* "change their mind" at an upper-level of *Alpha-Thought*, then indeed, *processing* wouldn't be necessary. But that is not the general experience of *Life*.

Systematic Processing is intended to assist a *Seeker* in eliminating the *barriers* of their own *"blindness"* or *"spiritual occlusion"* — meaning their *unreality* or *unknowingness* on the *reality-agreements* they've previously *agreed* to.

In the end: a *fragmented individual* is working against themselves in this *Universe*—working against their own former *agreements*. This only furthers the *solidity* of, and entrapment of a personal *viewpoint* within, this *Universe*.

42

Using *force* against *force*, *energy* against *energy*, only strengthens the *reality* of this *existence*; whereas true *Alpha-Thought* requires no *"force"* or *"energy"* to *"postulate/create"* something into being.

Our previous example regarding our *"wall"* exercise is quite apt, because it also represents a *"physical barrier."* After making *agreements* for the *reality* of *solid-matter* and a dependency on *viewpoints* attached to *physical eyes* (of a *body*), the *wall* represents a *barrier* to the total potential freedoms available. This is what makes receiving accurate *perceptions* from *"remote" viewpoints* (*ZU-Vision*) difficult for those individuals that continue to *compulsively create* and *unknowingly agree* to the *reality* of the *wall* as a *real barrier* for *Self.*

There are other *agreed-upon barriers* of a *Shared Universe* as well, less obvious perhaps, such as *"space"* —which is also to say *"distance."* And if there is to be any

43

creation or *activity* within this *"space,"* then there is also the observable factor of *"time"* — particularly when there is a perceived *motion* across *"distances"* (or even inherently in the "decay" or "erosion" of what is considered *solid-matter*).

For example: *communication* is a relay or motion of a "particle" or "bit" from *"Spot-A"* to *"Spot-B."* It must *"cross a distance"* and thus there is some *"time-lag"* in this action. It would be instantaneous were it not for the perception of some kind of *barrier*, such as *distance*. Without a *spatial distance*, however, there would be no *"Spot-A"* or *"Spot-B"* since the two would be indistinguishable and now essentially the same "spot."

There is a systematic relationship between *communication* and *"proximity"* (or *"closeness"*). This is reflected in the degree of *"likingness"* or *"affinity"* that is shared between ourselves and other individuals and things.

44

What we *"like,"* we generally want to keep *"closer"* to us; and the more we engage in *true communication* with someone, the more we can get to *liking* them, come into *closer "agreement"* with them (and be even further inclined to *communicate* with them more). We are, of course, only describing a systematic tendency in this case, not an absolute.

But these "factors" of *communication, likingness* and *agreement* are indeed interconnected; and that is how the area of *"barriers"* is initially handled at this *systematic processing level.* What is *"fragmentation,"* but an *energetic-mass;* and what is an *"energetic-mass,"* in an otherwise clear flow or current, but a *"barrier."*

For training and demonstration purposes, it may be helpful to *imagine* these *three factors* as a "current-flow" or "channel" connected between all individuals and things in existence. The "degree," "type," or "intensity" of these *flows* tends

45

to rise or fall collectively. Individuals *communicate*, they *like* each other, and *agree* with each other, *&tc.*, or else they "break," "reject," or otherwise "wall up" against these connections.

It is true that we may initially have "good reason" for establishing *"breaks"* and *"barriers."* However, we also have that interrelationship of factors (*communication, likingness,* and *agreement*) to be concerned with. This means by "cutting" *communication*, one then deals with *dislike* and *disagreement, &tc.* And there is the potential for an *automatic* (or *compulsive*) continuation of a *"break"* or *"barrier" unknowingly*.

More importantly is the fact that when the "event" or "incident" that prompted the *break* is not properly *confronted "As-It-Is,"* then *fragmentation* generally ensues. This means there is a potential for *turbulent emotional* or *mental "charge"* in that entire area thereafter. And this increas-

46

ingly builds up as *"chain of fragmentation"* connected to other similar "incidents."

For example: an individual that has often had their *affections* (*likingness*) "rejected" is likely to be more emotionally sensitive to that area, or more turbulently reactive at even the most subtle indications of "rejection" in the future. Our systematic solution is to handle the considerations from earlier "rejections" (which is where the primary *fragmentation* or "upset" is actually stemming from).

Breaks and *barriers* (in our three *flow-factors*) can occur from "enforcement" in addition to "rejecting" or "inhibiting" something. "Too much" of something is often just as uncomfortable as its "absence." This includes any time "too much" *force* is applied to any of our *flow-factors*—such as being *"forced to agree."* Quickly, we will shut down *communication flows*, then strongly *dislike* and *disagree* and so on as a cycle.

47

We say that this type of *fragmentation* occurs as a "chain" that is connected to many incidents—not just the one that *"triggered"* or *"restimulated"* a *reaction.* Usually the *reaction* is also out of "proportion" to what the present incident called for. But in essence, that is not *all* that the individual is *reacting* to; there is an entire "chain" of *fragmentation* accumulated from our past (or *"Backtrack"*) that is also now "active" and present.

The systematic solution to these types of "upsets" is to *"spot"* the underlying source of *fragmentation* that has *"resurfaced"* (or is *"in restimulation"*). This actually increases *"Actualized Awareness"* when one is "upset"—as opposed to trying to get someone to "calm down," which is really only a *"suppression"* (and which only further validates and strengthens the *fragmentation* itself).

Systematic Processing in these areas is most effective when the *earliest* incident of a certain type of occurrence can be *spotted*. For a *Seeker's* first cycle through the lessons of the *Professional Course*, only those events taking place during *this* lifetime are *processed* (unless additional data is already readily available); however, in later passes through our *course* material, an advanced application would include "past lives" ("*Backtrack*") too.

DEFRAGMENTING THE "FACTORS"

We have, for our *systematic processing*, three "factors" (or *flow-factors*) that require *defragmentation*: "*communication*," "*likingness*" and "*agreement*." There are also two basic *flow-types* applied to each *factor*: "*insistence*" (or "*enforcement*") and "*rejection*" (or "*inhibition*").

The three *processing command-lines* ("PCL") for each of the following *processes*

49

are *run* in alternation until any sense of *"fragmented energetic charge"* (concerning an area) has fallen away or dispersed. *Run* as many of the *processes* within a single *session* as can be handled—being certain to *end-the-session* when "feeling good" and alert. All of these *processes* employ the *"Analytical Recall"* technique (as first described in *Lesson-2* of this *Professional Course*).

As an additional point of instruction: if any of the *processes* stirs up significant *energetic turbulence*, a more complete *defragmentation* will only occur if an *earlier* instance of a similar type is *spotted*. This may, in fact, have to continue "down a chain" of *even earlier* instances until the *earliest* one available for *recall* is *spotted*. Only then can the actual *fragmented imprint* (underlying the "upset") be handled and *confronted*. Also be sure to *notice* some "things" and "actions" within the incident, rather than simply listing it off as *recalled*.

50

PROCESSING SECTION

Communication Factor:
Enforced Out-Flows

1. *"Recall a time when you insisted that someone communicate with someone (or something)."*

2. *"Recall a time when someone insisted that you communicate with someone (or something)."*

3. *"Recall a time when someone insisted others communicate with someone (or something)."*

Communication Factor:
Enforced In-Flows

1. *"Recall a time when you insisted that someone communicate with you."*

2. *"Recall a time when someone insisted that you communicate with them."*

3. *"Recall a time when someone insisted that others communicate with them."*

Communication Factor:
Inhibited Out-Flows

1. *"Recall a time when you insisted that someone not communicate with someone (or something)."*

2. *"Recall a time when someone insisted that you not communicate with something (or someone)."*

3. *"Recall a time when someone insisted that others not communicate with someone (or something)."*

Communication Factor:
Inhibited In-Flows

1. *"Recall a time when you rejected someone's communication."*

2. *"Recall a time when someone rejected your communication."*

3. *"Recall a time when someone rejected another's communication."*

Communication Factor: Clear-Flow

1. *"Recall a time when you communicated well with someone."*

2. *"Recall a time when someone communicated well with you."*

3. *"Recall a time when someone communicated well with others."*

Likingness Factor: Enforced Out-Flows

1. *"Recall a time when you insisted that someone like something (or someone)."*

2. *"Recall a time when someone insisted that you like something (or someone)."*

3. *"Recall a time when someone insisted others like something (or someone)."*

Likingness Factor: Enforced In-Flows

1. *"Recall a time when you insisted that someone like you."*

2. *"Recall a time when someone insisted that you like them."*

3. *"Recall a time when someone insisted that others like them."*

Likingness Factor: Inhibited Out-Flows

1. *"Recall a time when you insisted that someone dislike something (or someone)."*

2. *"Recall a time when someone insisted that you dislike something (or someone)."*

3. *"Recall a time when someone insisted that others dislike something (or someone)."*

Likingness Factor: Inhibited In-Flows

1. *"Recall a time when you rejected someone's affection (or attention)."*

2. *"Recall a time when someone rejected your affection (or attention)."*

3. *"Recall a time when someone rejected another's affection (or attention)."*

Likingness Factor: Clear-Flow

1. *"Recall a time when you liked someone."*

2. *"Recall a time when someone liked you."*

3. *"Recall a time when someone liked another."*

Agreement Factor: Enforced Out-Flows

1. *"Recall a time when you insisted that someone agree with something (or someone)."*

2. *"Recall a time when someone insisted that you agree with something (or someone)."*

3. *"Recall a time when someone insisted others agree with something (or someone)."*

Agreement Factor: Enforced In-Flows

1. *"Recall a time when you insisted that someone agree with you."*

2. *"Recall a time when someone insisted that you agree with them."*

3. *"Recall a time when someone insisted that others agree with them."*

Agreement Factor: Inhibited Out-Flows

1. *"Recall a time when you insisted that someone disagree with something (or someone)."*

2. *"Recall a time when someone insisted that you disagree with something (or someone)."*

3. *"Recall a time when someone insisted others disagree with something (or someone)."*

Agreement Factor: Inhibited In-Flows

1. *"Recall a time when you rejected someone's reality (or refused to agree with them)."*

2. *"Recall a time when someone rejected your reality (or refused to agree with you)."*

3. *"Recall a time when someone rejected another's reality (or refused to agree with them)."*

Agreement Factor: Clear-Flow

1. *"Recall a time when you agreed with someone."*

2. *"Recall a time when someone agreed with you."*

3. *"Recall a time when someone agreed with another."*

HANDLING THE "FLOW-FACTORS"

Very early on the *"Backtrack,"* we approached existence from a much more *"All-Pervading"* and *"All-Knowing"* state—but, of course, that did not offer us much room to experience any kind of *game-conditions.* Therefore, to have some genuine sense of *interest* or *curiosity* in our lives, it was necessary for us to first *agree* to *"Not-Know"* at least *something* about something.

Where it comes to our encounters in this present *Shared-Game Universe*, the *"Not-Knowing"* is what allows the original *barriers* to exist. The *agreed-upon* boundaries defined (for example) by an individual's own *"Mind"* or a *"Wall"* restrict the *apparent* "ALL-ness" that could be potentially experienced or *Known.* These *barriers* only exist, of course, within the

57

"*reality*" of the *Game* or *Universe*; they are not "*actual*" conditions.

Most of the time, the "upsets" and "imbalances" that affect us in our daily lives come from the *perception* that there are too many *factor-breaks* and *barriers*. An individual can also become "inhibited," "antagonistic" or "bored" by not having enough *randomness* too. Therefore, a happy healthy life is comprised of just enough "*game*" for one's own *tolerance*. Of course, increasing that *tolerance* is quite desirable for *Ascension*.

We often approach the *Game of Life*, then, from some degree of "*Not-Knowing*." Our *attention* is then directed by *interest* or *curiosity*. This generates an *energy-flow*, such as we have described in our lessons concerning the *factors*, *flow-types* and *circuits*. When there is "good" *communication* and *agreement* (*&tc.*), life plays out with minimal disruption and difficulty.

But, *this Universe* is quite obviously not built upon *Self-Honesty*—and *fragmentation* runs rampant in the typical *"Human"* experience. Often times, an individual does not fully *"connect"* and instead encounters some degree of *resistance*. Assuming one continues to be *interested* in spite of this, an increase or amplification (intensity) of the *energy-flow* (or *attention-flow*) is necessary to overcome the *resistance.* This is where the individual tends to find some trouble.

As we have spoken of previously in this lesson, when an individual starts to apply *energy* against *energy,* and *force* against *force,* they begin to engage with further *barriers* and more solid *game-conditions.* In the example just given: if an *interest* or *curiosity* (in someone or something) is *inhibited*, it promotes an *increased desire* and a more impactful (or solid) energetic or material *effort* to overcome the *resistance.* This brings us far and below the operat-

59

ing levels of high-power *Alpha-Thought* and true *Self-determinism*.

Continuing our example: if the individual is unsuccessful in accomplishing what they *desire*, and is unable (or unwilling) to abandon the pursuit, the directed energy (of the flow) must increase further in its material solidity, and *effort* will now be applied to *enforce* or *insist upon* the intended *flow*. This is when an individual falls low enough in *Awareness* to start operating *automatically* on *reactive-mechanisms* (*fragmentation*).

Once an individual starts *reactively* operating on *fragmentation*, their *efforts* generally are unsuccessful—quite frankly because they are intensely applying *effort* in the first place. Assuming this fails to deliver the *desired results* (or *effect*), as it usually does, the individual switches to the *inhibition* side of the *flow*. The "thing" or "person" (*terminal*) is now so "*highly charged*" that the *intentional effort* becomes "to get away" from it (or to "keep it away"). But, the individual is still *intensely* and *compulsively* "connected" to it.

Rather than confronting a thing *"As-It-Is,"* the typical *reactive-response* to "getting away from" something that is *highly charged* (or undesirable) is to "make nothing" of *it*—to treat it as if it were "not a thing." It is no longer experienced *"As-It-Is,"* and yet there is still a *"flow"* that an individual now starts rejecting furiously. This is the point when one angrily "doesn't want" anything to do with the thing they formerly *desired.* And in low-level cases, the individual will go as far as to act out against (or even destroy) it.

This systematic sequence we have described may apply to any of the three *flow-factors.* This is the theory demonstrated in the *processes* found in the previous section—which provides a systematic means of sorting out the originating source of *turbulence* and *fragmentation* for such *flows* encountered in everyday life.

When the *Alpha-Spirit* decides to *"Not-Know"* something in order to have a "game"—an application of *attention* and *interest* (or *curiosity*) is what essentially provides something to "do" ("be" or "have") in existence. It provides enough *randomness* for one to enjoy their life. However, when this is not handled properly—or when the "player" is not operating clearly in *Self-Honesty*—succumbing to a level of *intense desire* only imposes further *fragmentation* and *barriers*. Life suddenly becomes more difficult to manage.

The "upsets" of life are treated as *breaks* (or *barriers*) in the *flow-factors*. For *Solo-Processing*, a *Seeker* first looks over the *incident* or *occurrence* carefully, *spotting* and *confronting* whatever is accessible. To make the *fragmentation* available for *processing*, the first step is simply seeing

"What-Is," and not focusing on any *confusions* or other unresolved parts of the experience.

These *flow-factor "upsets"* are only *systematically processed* when a *Seeker* is distanced from the source of the *break*—when the *turbulence* is not actively *restimulated* by the environment. If a *Seeker* is still too *emotionally charged-up* (hysterically upset, *&tc.*) from a recent *occurrence,* then the first step must include alternating *"spotting something in the incident"* and *"spotting something in the (room)"* until further *processing* can begin.

When the *Seeker* is ready for *defragmentation* of the *upset,* the instructions are: consider each of the *flow-factors*—*"communication," "likingness"* and *"agreement"*—and determine which was the most significantly present in the *upset.* Once you have spotted the *factor,* consider what *flow-type* is attached to it; primarily, is it being *"enforced"* or *"inhibited"*?

Familiarity with PCL from the previous section should help you to identify the "quality" of the particular *flow* you are handling for this form of *processing*. Note that in this lesson, we have also added *"Not-Knowing," "interest/curiosity"* and *"desire"* to this "scale" of potential *flow-types.* These other three types are sequentially "above" (or precede) *"enforcement," "inhibition"* and *"refusal"* on the "scale."

When the correct combination of *factor* and *flow-type* is *spotted* for an *upset*, there should be some sense of *relief* or *emotional release.* If not, it is possible that either the *factor* or *flow-type* (or both) was assessed wrongly. In that case, you simply return to the beginning of these steps and try again. If you "stir" up too much *turbulence* in trying to find out, simply add the alternating PCL of *"spotting something in the room,"* so that not all of your attention is fixed on the *restimulation* of the *upset.*

The *relief/release* gained by this *spotting* technique (above) may be partial or complete. If it's complete, then you can move off onto another *process*, or *end-session*. If, however, it is only partially *defragmented* (but there is some *relief* from *spotting* the correct *factor* and *flow-type*), then you continue with additional steps (below).

First, *spot* the "*flow-direction*" or "*circuit.*" For example: did *you inhibit* someone's *communication*, or did someone else *inhibit yours*? Then, *spot* exactly what "*communication*" was *inhibited* (for example); and then *spot* what you "did" (*action*) and what you "decided" (*thought*) in the incident. If possible, also *spot* any lingering upper-level *considerations* and *postulates* you made as a result of the experience.

If this technique doesn't provide a complete *defragmentation*, it is likely that there is an *earlier incident* of a similar nature that is connected to it "on a chain." All you need to do is *spot* the *earlier incident* and *run* through the steps again.

If at any time during this *processing*, things seem to "feel better" and then suddenly the *fragmentation* seems "more solid" again, you likely *ran* the *process* too long. Simply alternate: *spotting* the moment you had experienced the *end-point,* and *spotting* something in the room, until you get to "feeling better" again.

MORE ON "BARRIERS"

Let us now take a moment and examine a holistic view, reviewing what we have *realized,* from all the lessons composing our *Professional Course* for the "*Pathway to Ascension*" so far.

In the beginning, an *Alpha-Spirit* goes "*out-of-communication*" *knowingly* and *selectively.* While this, at first, is a matter of personal preference or choice, it is generally encouraged or influenced from an "outside" or "other-determined" source. This is undesirable, because once an individual goes *"out-of-communication"* too far, they then are suddenly easier to *control* from outside "environmental" and "other-determined" sources.

Once a being is *"out-of-communication"* there is a greater chance for encountering things that they don't *like*; and the individual begins *protesting* them, instead of *confronting* them. This is when *fragmentation* sets in; the individual starts to *compulsively create* (and *"postulate"*) things into existence from a state of *protest* (as in *"communicating"* a *protest*)—and this leads to the experience of *problems*.

In typical cases of *fragmentation* (*e.g. the Human Condition*), an individual experiencing *"problems"* will apply increasingly low-level *efforts* to "solve" the *problem*. This leads to committing *"Harmful-Acts,"*

67

which now have to be *held-out* (and other actions that are now consciously *held-back*), leading to only further and further *withdrawal* from existence *"As-It-Is"* and the development of additional *barriers*, such as we have described throughout this lesson.

More *recently* on the *Backtrack*, an *Alpha-Spirit* identifies *Self* more closely as a "material body" that can be hurt (because *Self* "considers" that *Self* can be hurt as a result). Prior to this, earlier in the *game*, the *Alpha-Spirits* were more like *"demi-gods"* that could really only annoy or tease one another—or mess up each others *creations*. But while *knowingly* operating as an *"eternal being,"* they knew that nothing permanent could affect each other.

Of course, we have fallen quite far in our *Awareness* of this native state, and have found ourselves essentially "stuck" within these *creations*.

From the perspective of the *Human Condition*, it often *appears* as though we have "good reason" for the various *upsets* we encounter in life—especially since our recent history on the *Backtrack* has included great "pain" and "destruction." It *appears* as though the *breaks* and *barriers* (of *factors* and *flows*) are a direct result from the various harms that have been present in this lifetime and in recorded history.

The truth is that these *breaks* and *barriers* are connected to "chains" of *fragmentation* that occurred much earlier in our *Spiritual Timeline* (or *Backtrack*); back when we were still "above" the level of *considering* ourselves able to be actually harmed (in a mortal sense). We could, however, still feel "hurt" from, for example, *"refusal to communicate"* or *"rejected affections,"* *&tc.* That is how a lot of the "mess" in existence came into being: first the *breaks* and *barriers*, and then the *"wars."*

At first, a *Seeker* may question the *systematic accuracy* of the *"fragmentation pattern"* we have just described. After all, personal tastes (*"likes"*) often differ, and there are many people presently not *"communicating"* with each other—and this does not seem to present a *problem* or *upset* in itself. But, that is not what we mean in this lesson. Simply not having a lot of *flow-activity* is not the same as having a *factor-break*, in that it does not carry the *"emotional charge"* or a *"chain of fragmentation"* with it.

The *factor-breaks* we experience in this lifetime as *upsets* only occur because there is already existing *"charge"* or *"fragmentation"* present on the line. A proper or "clear" use of the *factors* is usually sufficient to "dissipate" or "eliminate" most of what accumulates in everyday life. For example: when we "listen to," "care for," "help," or otherwise engage well with others and our environment, our lives bring "happiness."

On the other hand, when the *factor-flows* are "cut" or "broken" abruptly—either by *enforcement* or *inhibition*—any of the "charge" that would be "relieved" by a proper *flow,* suddenly "backs up" (or becomes a "blockage") as an *energetic-mass.* This is what prompts a personal response, originating from the *reactive-mechanisms* of *fragmentation*, that seem so excessively out of proportion to what a present situation calls for.

As we close this lesson, it is important to understand: it is not the *factor-flows* themselves that cause *fragmented charge* on one's track, but an individual's own *compulsions* and *inhibitions* in regards to the *breaks* and *barriers* encountered. And this includes the *fragmentation* encountered concerning what an individual "must" or "must not" *Be, do* or *have.* And this returns us full circle to what we have covered in the earlier lessons regarding *"reach"* and *"withdrawal."*

71

Finally, it is only when we are in a state of Self-Honesty, with a *willingness* to *Be*, *do*, or *have* "anything" (without any *compulsion* or *reactive avoidance*), that we are truly *free* of the *Human Condition*—having risen far beyond the *barriers* of *upsets* and *problems* inherent in that *fragmented* state.

It is only when we can regain the high-power *Alpha-Thought* of our former native state that we will have a truly *Self-determined* and totally *free choice*. In a *fragmented state*, all *considerations* are of a "lower order" because the external "other-determined" factors of life are given more validation as a *source* of our experience of existence than we give ourselves. This is one of the things that improves for a *Seeker* as they progress in their *processing levels* of *Systemology* and prepare *Self* to again experience an *Ascended* state.

ADVANCED PROCESSING

The following *systematic processes* are traditionally applied after using the PCL given in *Lesson-6*: "*Spot three places you are not.*" The purpose is to more easily assume a *viewpoint* that is "*exterior*" to the *body* (or even the confines of the *Physical Universe*) and be able to "*spot*" things from that *viewpoint.*

For these *processes*, simply *imagine* that you are hovering above, and freely able to move about, a city or populated area. At this *processing level*, we are not concerned with how accurate or vivid these "*remote*" perceptions (or "*ZU-Vision*") may be. Just "*spot*" things anyway; *imagining* them (or how they *might* be) as needed.

Attacking

1. "*Spot three people that you are not attacking.*"

73

2. *"Spot three people that are not attacking you."*

3. *"Spot three people that are not attacking others."*

Hatred

1. *"Spot three people that you do not hate."*

2. *"Spot three people that do not hate you."*

3. *"Spot three people that don't hate each other."*

Ordering

1. *"Spot three people that you are not giving orders to."*

2. *"Spot three people that are not giving you orders."*

3. *"Spot three people that aren't giving orders to others."*

Beauty

1. *"Spot three things you find beautiful to look at."*

2. *"Spot three things someone else would find beautiful to look at."*

3. *"Spot three people looking at beautiful things."*

Safety

1. *"Spot three places where your body would be safe."*

2. *"Spot three places where someone else would be safe."*

3. *"Spot three places where other bodies would be safe."*

0. *"Spot three places where you would be safe."*

The Systemology Professional Course
continues in the next lesson booklet:
CONQUEST OF ILLUSION

GLOSSARY

actualization : to make actual, not just potential; to bring into full solid Reality; to realize fully in *Awareness* as a "thing."

agreement (reality) : unanimity of opinion of what is "thought" to be known; an accepted arrangement of how things are; things we consider as "real" or as an "is" of "reality"; a consensus of what is real as made by standard-issue (common) participants; what an individual contributes to or accepts as "real"; in *Systemology*, a synonym for "*reality.*"

alpha : the first, primary, basic, superior or beginning of some form; in *Systemology*, referring to the state of existence operating on spiritual archetypes and postulates, will and intention "exterior" to the low-level condensation and solidarity of energy and matter as the 'physical universe' (*beta*).

alpha-spirit : a "spiritual" *Life*-form; the "true" *Self* or I-AM; the *individual*; the spiritual (*alpha*) *Self* that is animating the (*beta*) physical body or "*genetic vehicle*" using a continuous *Lifeline* of spiritual ("*ZU*") energy; an individu-

76

al spiritual (*alpha*) entity possessing no physical mass or measurable waveform (motion) in the Physical Universe as itself, so it animates the (*beta*) physical body or "*genetic vehicle*" as a catalyst to experience *Self*-determined causality in effect within the *Physical Universe*; a singular unit or point of *Spiritual Awareness* that is *Aware* that it is *Aware*.

alpha thought : the highest spiritual *Self-determination* over creation and existence exercised by an Alpha-Spirit; the Alpha range of pure *Creative Ability* based on direct postulates and considerations of *Beingness*; spiritual qualities comparable to "thought" but originating in Alpha-existence, independently superior to a Mind-System.

ascension : actualized *Awareness* elevated to the point of true "spiritual existence" exterior to *beta existence*. An "Ascended Master" is one who has returned to an incarnation on Earth as an inherently *Enlightened One*, demonstrable in their words and actions; they have the ability to *Self-direct* the "Mind" and "Body" as *Self* (as a "Spirit"); and to maintain consciousness as a personal identity continuum with the same *Self-directed* control and communication of Will-Intention that is exercised, actualized and developed deliberately during one's present incarnation.

associative knowledge : significance or meaning of a facet or aspect assigned to (or considered to have) a direct relationship with another facet; to connect or relate ideas or facets of existence with one another; in traditional systems logic, an equivalency of significance or meaning between facets or sets that are grouped together, such as in $(a + b) + c = a + (b + c)$; in Systemology, erroneous associative knowledge is assignment of the same value to all facets or parts considered as related (even when they are not actually so), such as in $a = a, b = a, c = a$ and so forth without distinction.

attention : active use of *Awareness* toward a specific aspect or thing; the act of "attending" with the presence of *Self*; a direction of focus or concentration of *Awareness* along a particular channel or conduit or toward a particular terminal node or communication termination point; the Self-directed concentration of personal energy as a combination of observation, thought-waves and consideration; focused application of *Self-Directed Awareness*.

awareness : the highest sense of-and-as *Self* in knowing and being as I-AM (the *Alpha-Spirit*); the extent of beingness directed as a viewpoint (POV) experienced by *Self* as *Knowingness*.

beta (existence) : all manifestation in the "Physical Universe" (KI, in *Zuism*); the conditions of *Awareness* for the *Alpha-spirit* (*Self*) as a physical organic *Lifeform* or "*genetic vehicle*" in which it experiences causality in the *Physical Universe*.

charge : to fill or furnish with a quality; to supply with energy; to lay a command upon; in *Systemology*—to imbue with intention; to overspread with emotion; personal energy stores and significances entwined as fragmentation in mental images, reactive-response encoding and intellectual (and/or) programmed beliefs.

circuit : a circular path or loop; a closed-path within a system that allows a flow; a pattern or action or wave movement that follows a specific route or potential path only; in *Systemology*, "*communication processing*" pertaining to a specific *flow* of energy or information along a channel; "*feedback loop.*"

communication : successful transmission of information, data, energy (&tc.) along a message line, with a reception of feedback; an energetic flow of intention to cause an effect (or duplication) at a distance; the personal energy moved or acted upon by will or else 'selective directed attention'; the 'messenger action' used to trans-

79

mit and receive energy across a medium; also relay of energy, a message or signal—or even locating a personal POV (viewpoint) for the Self—along the *ZU-line*.

confront : to come around in front of; to be in the presence of; to stand in front of, or in the face of; to meet "face-to-face" or "face-up-to"; additionally, in *Systemology*, to fully tolerate or acceptably withstand an encounter with a particular manifestation without an automatic reactive response..

consideration : careful analytical reflection of all aspects; deliberation; determining the significance of a "thing" in relation to similarity or dissimilarity to other "things"; evaluation of facts and importance of certain facts; thorough examination of all aspects related to, or important for, making a decision; the analysis of consequences and estimation of significance when making decisions; also in *Systemology*, the *postulate* or *Alpha-Thought* that defines the state of *beingness* for what something "*is.*"

defragmentation : the *reparation* of wholeness; collecting all dispersed parts to reform an original whole; a process of removing "*fragmentation*" in data or knowledge to provide a clear understanding; applying techniques and processes that promote a *holistic* interconnected *al-*

pha state, favoring observational *Awareness* of continuity in all spiritual and physical systems; in *Systemology*, a "*Seeker*" achieving actualized "*Self-Honest Awareness*" is said to be in a basic state of *beta-defragmentation*, whereas *Alpha-defragmentation* is the rehabilitation of the *creative ability*, managing the *Spiritual Timeline* and the POV of *Self* as Alpha-Spirit (I-AM).

fragmentation : breaking into parts and scattering the pieces; the *fractioning* of wholeness or the *fracture* of a holistic interconnected *alpha* state, favoring observational *Awareness* of perceived connectivity between parts; *discontinuity*; separation of a totality into parts; in *Systemology*, a person outside of *Self-Honesty* is said to be operating from a *fragmented* state.

flow : movement across (or through) a channel (or conduit); a direction of active energetic motion, typically distinguished as either an *in-flow*, *out-flow* or *cross-flow*.

genetic-vehicle : a physical *Life*-form; the physical (*beta*) body that is animated/controlled by the (*Alpha*) *Spirit* using a continuous *Spiritual Lifeline* (ZU); a physical (*beta*) organic receptacle and catalyst for the (*Alpha*) *Self* to operate "causes" and experience "effects" within the *Physical Universe*.

harmful-act : a counter-survival mode of behavior or action (esp. that causes harm to one of more *Spheres of Existence*)—or—an overtly aggressive (hostile and/or destructive) action against an individual or any other *Sphere of Existence*; in *Utilitarian Systemology*—a short-sighted (serves fewest/lowest *Spheres of Existence*) intentional overtly harmful action to resolve a perceived problem; a revision of the rule for standard *Utilitarianism* for Systemology to distinguish actions which provide the least benefit to the least number of *Spheres of Existence*, or else the greatest harm to the greatest number of *Spheres of Existence*; in *moral philosophy*—an action which can be experienced by few and/or which one would not be willing to experience for themselves (*theft, slander, rape, &tc*); an iniquity or iniquitous act.

hold-back : withheld communications (esp. actions) such as "*Hold-Outs*"; intentional (or automatic) withdrawal (as opposed to reach); Self-restraint (which may eventually be enforced or automated); not reaching, acting or expressing, when one should be; an ability that is now restrained (on automatic) due to inability to withhold it on Self-determinism alone.

hold-outs : in photography, the numerous snapshots/pictures withheld from the final display or

82

professional presentation of the event; withheld communications; in Utilitarian Systemology—energetic withdrawal and communication breaks with a "*terminal*" and its *Sphere of Existence* as a result of a "*Harmful-Act*"; unspoken or undiscovered (hidden, covert) actions that an individual withholds communications of, fearing punishment or endangerment of *Self-preservation* (*First Sphere*); the act of hiding (or keeping hidden) the truth of a "*Harmful-Act*"; a refusal to communicate with a *Pilot*; also "*Hold-Back.*"

holistic : the examination of interconnected systems as encompassing something greater than the *sum* of their "parts."

Human Condition : a standard default state of Human experience that is generally accepted to be the extent of its potential identity (*beingness*) —currently treated as *Homo Sapiens Sapiens,* but which is scheduled for replacement by *Homo Novus* (the "New Human").

imprint : to strongly impress, stamp, mark (or outline) onto a softer 'impressible' substance; to mark with pressure onto a surface; in *Systemology*, used to indicate permanent Reality impressions marked by frequencies, energies or interactions experienced during periods of emotional distress, pain, unconsciousness, loss, enforcement, or something antagonistic to

83

physical (personal) survival, all of which are are stored with other reactive response-mechanisms at lower-levels of *Awareness* as opposed to the active memory database and proactive processing center of the Mind; an experiential "memory-set" that may later resurface—be triggered or stimulated artificially—as Reality, of which similar responses will be engaged automatically; holographic-like imagery "stamped" onto consciousness as composed of energetic *facets* tied to the "snap-shot" of an experience.

invalidate : decrease the level or degree or *agreement* as Reality.

pilot : a professional steersman responsible for healthy functional operation of a ship toward a specific destination; in *Systemology*, an intensive trained individual qualified to specially apply *Systemology Processing* to assist other *Seekers* on the *Pathway*.

point-of-view (POV) : a point to view from; an opinion or attitude as expressed from a specific identity-phase; a specific standpoint or vantage-point; a definitive manner of consideration specific to an individual phase or identity; a place or position affording a specific view or vantage; circumstances and programming of an individual that is conducive to a particular response, consideration or belief-set (paradigm); a position (consideration) or place (location) that provides a specific view or perspective (subjective) on experience (of the objective).

postulate : to put forward as truth; to suggest or assume an existence *to be*; to state or affirm the existence of particular conditions; to provide a basis of reasoning and belief; a basic theory accepted as fact; in *Systemology*, Alpha-Thought —the top-most decisions or considerations made by the Alpha-Spirit regarding the "*is-ness*" (what things "are") about energy-matter and space-time.

presence : a quality of some thing (*energy/matter*) being "present" in space-time; personal orientation of *Self* as an *Awareness* (*POV*) located in present space-time (environment) and communicating with extant energy-matter.

processing command line (PCL) or **command line** : a directed input; a specific command using highly selective language for *Systemology Processing*; a predetermined directive statement (cause) intended to focus concentrated attention (effect).

processing, systematic : the inner-workings or "through-put" result of systems; in *Systemology*, a method of applied spiritual technology used toward personal Self-Actualization; methods of selective directed attention, communicated language and associative imagery that increases personal control of the human condition.

realization : the clear perception of an understanding; a consideration or understanding on what is "actual"; to make "real" or give "reality" to so as to grant a property of "beingness" or "being as it is"; the state or instance of coming to an *Awareness*; in *Systemology*, "gnosis" or true knowledge achieved during *systematic processing*; achievement of a new (or higher) cognition, true knowledge or perception of Self; a consideration of reality or assignment of meaning.

responsibility : the *ability* to *respond*; the extent of mobilizing *power* and *understanding* an individual maintains as *Awareness* to enact *change*; the proactive ability to *Self-direct* and make decisions independent of an outside authority.

Seeker : an individual on the *Pathway to Self-Honesty*; a practitioner of *Mardukite Systemology* or *Systemology Processing*, that is working toward *Spiritual Ascension*.

Self-actualization : bringing the full potential of the Human spirit into Reality; expressing full capabilities and creativeness of the *Alpha-Spirit*.

Self-determinism : the freedom to act, clear of external control or influence; the personal control of Will to direct intention.

Self-honesty : the basic or original *alpha* state of *being* and *knowing*; clear and present total *Awareness* of-and-as *Self*, in its most basic and true proactive expression of itself as *Spirit* or *I-AM*—free of artificial attachments, perceptive filters and other emotionally-reactive or mentally-conditioned programming imposed on the human condition by the systematized physical world; the ability to experience existence without judgment.

spiritual timeline : a continuous stream of moment-to-moment *Mental Images* (or a record of experiences) that defines the "past" of a spiritual being (or *Alpha-Spirit*) and which includes impressions (*imprints, &tc.*) from all life-incarnations and significant spiritual events the being has encountered; in Systemology, also "*backtrack.*"

Spheres of Existence : a series of *eight* concentric circles, rings or spheres (each larger than the former) that is overlaid onto the Standard Model of Beta-Existence to demonstrate the dynamic systems of existence extending out from the POV of Self (often as a "body") at the *First Sphere*; these are given in the basic eightfold systems as: *Self, Home/Family, Groups, Humanity, Life on Earth, Physical Universe, Spiritual Universe* and *Infinity-Divinity.*

Systemology : a modern tradition of applied religious philosophy and spiritual technology based on *Arcane Tablets* (in combination with "*general systemology*" and "*games theory*") developed in the New Age underground by Joshua Free in 2011 as an advanced futurist extension of the *Mardukite Research Org.*; also known as "*Mardukite Systemology,*" "*Metahuman Systemology*" and "*Spiritual Systemology.*"

terminal (node) : a point, end, or mass, on a line; a connection point for closing an electric circuit, such as a post on a battery terminating at each end of its own systematic function; a point of connectivity with other points; in systems, a contact point of interaction; a point of interaction with other points.

turbulence : a quality or state of distortion or disturbance that creates irregularity of a flow or pattern; the quality or state of aberration on a line (such as ragged edges) or the emotional "turbulent feelings" attached to a particular flow or terminal node; a violent, haphazard or disharmonious commotion (such as in the ebb of gusts and lulls of wind action).

validation : a reinforcement of agreements or considerations as being "real."

viewpoint : see *"point-of-view" (POV).*

willingness : the state of conscious Self-determined ability and interest (directed attention) to *Be*, *Do* or *Have*; a Self-determined consideration to reach, face up to (*confront*) or manage some "mass" or energy; the extent to which an individual considers themselves able to participate, act or communicate along some line, to put attention or intention on the line, or to produce (create) an effect.

ZU : the ancient Sumerian cuneiform sign for the archaic verb—*"to know," "knowingness"* or *"awareness"*; in *Mardukite Zuism and Systemology*, the active energy/matter of the "Spiritual Universe" (AN) experienced as a *Lifeforce* or *consciousness* that imbues living forms extant in the "Physical Universe" (KI); *"Spiritual Life Energy"*; energy demonstrated by the WILL of an actualized *Alpha-Spirit* in the "Spiritual Universe" (AN), which impinges its *Awareness* into the Physical Universe (KI), animating/controlling *Life* for its experience of *beta-existence* along an individual Alpha-Spirit's personal *Identity-continuum*, called a *ZU-line*.

***Zu*-Line** : a theoretical construct in *Mardukite*

Zuism and Systemology demonstrating *Spiritual Life Energy* (*ZU*) as a personal individual "continuum" of Awareness interacting with all Spheres of Existence on the Standard Model of Systemology; a spectrum of potential variations and interactions of a monistic continuum or singular *Spiritual Life Energy* demonstrated on the Standard Model; an energetic channel of potential POV and "locations" of Beingness, demonstrated in early Systemology materials as an individual Alpha-Spirit's personal *Identity- continuum*, potentially connecting *Awareness* of *Self* with "*Infinity*" simultaneous with all points considered in existence; a symbolic demonstration of the "*Life-line*" on which *Awareness (ZU)* extends from the direction of the "Spiritual Universe" (AN) in its true original *alpha state* through an entire possible range of activity resulting in its *beta state* and control of a *genetic-entity* occupying the *Physical Universe (KI)*.

Zu-Vision : the true and basic (*Alpha*) Point-of-View (perspective, POV) maintained by *Self* as *Alpha-Spirit* outside boundaries or considerations of the *Human Condition* and *exterior* to beta-existence reality agreements with the Physical Universe; a POV of Self *as* "a unit of Spiritual Awareness" that exists independent of a "body" and entrapment in a *Human Condition*; "spirit vision" in its truest sense.

90

Fundamentals of Systemology
in six
Basic Course Lesson Booklets

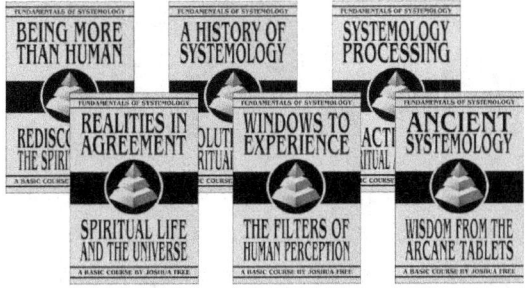

Also
available
as a
six-in-one
hardcover
edition!

THE SYSTEMOL

Seekers and students of the *Basic Course* and *Professional Course* will also be interested in the *Advanced Series* of the *Systemology Core.* These volumes are a complete chronological record of the Mardukite New Thought developments from the Systemology Society, published in 2019 through 2023.

The *Systemology Core* begins with the first professional publication released when the *Mardukite Systemology Society* emerged from the underground in 2019, with: *"The Tablets of Destiny Revelation."*

OGY PATHWAY

The Tablets of Destiny Revelation:
*How Long-Lost Anunnaki Wisdom
Can Change the Fate of Humanity*

Crystal Clear: *Handbook for Seekers*

Metahuman Destinations (2 *volumes*)

Imaginomicon:
Approaching Gateways to Higher Universes

Way of the Wizard: *Utilitarian Systemology*

Systemology-180: *Fast-Track to Ascension*

Systemology Backtrack:
Reclaiming Spiritual Power & Past-Life Memory

PUBLISHED BY THE **JOSHUA FREE** IMPRINT REPRESENTING

The Mardukite Academy of Systemology

THE JOSHUA FREE IMPRINT
JFI PUBLICATIONS

MARDUKITE
ZUISM

mardukite.com

www.ingramcontent.com/pod-product-compliance
Lightning Source LLC
Chambersburg PA
CBHW071212120626
46546CB00006B/2527